Small Fun Pets: Beginning Pets for Kids 9-12

Fun Pets For Kids Book 1

Jacquelyn Elnor Johnson

www.CrimsonHillBooks.com/best-pets-for-kids

© 2017 Crimson Hill Books/Crimson Hill Products Inc.

All rights reserved. No part of this book may be copied, lent, excerpted or quoted except in very brief passages by a reviewer.

Cataloguing in Publication Data

Jacquelyn Elnor Johnson

Small Fun Pets: Beginning Pets for Kids 9-12

Description: Crimson Hill Books trade hardcover edition | Nova Scotia, Canada

ISBN 978-1-988650-89-0 (Hardcover)

BISAC: JNF003170 Juvenile Nonfiction: Animals - Pets | JUV002190 Juvenile Fiction: Animals - Pets

THEMA: YNNH - Children's / Teenage general interest: Pets & pet care | YNN - Children's / Teenage general interest: Nature, animals, the natural world | YN - Children's / Teenage: general interest

Record available at https://www.bac-lac.gc.ca/eng/Pages/home.aspx

Cover design, Book design and formatting: Jesse Johnson

Crimson Hill Books

(a division of)

Crimson Hill Products Inc.

Wolfville, Nova Scotia

Canada

A young girl with her dog.

Photo by Ilipkind on Pixabay.

For Teachers and Parents

When kids think of pets, they think of fun.

But is the pet they want really the best pet for them? And for you?

Parents and teachers want children to get the pet that's:

- safe (for both pet and child),
- easy to care for and keep healthy, and
- pleasant to live with.

To be a best small pet for kids, this creature also needs to have simple care requirements that a child can manage with minimal adult supervision.

Most teachers and many parents also expect a beginner pet to be inexpensive both to buy and to maintain.

Children are focused on all the fun they'll soon be having with their new pet. They're excited that it will live in their room, or their classroom.

Adults want kids to enjoy pets, but they also want kids to gain the life lessons caring for a pet can provide. These are:

- taking responsibility,
- kindness to others,
- compassion, especially for those smaller than you,
- respect for our natural world, and another important life skill,
- cleaning up messes.

If this pet will live in a child's bedroom or in your classroom, it also must be reasonably quiet and content, most of the time.

So what pets are there that delight kids while meeting all the needs of teachers and parents?

Here are the best starter pets, plus a few that can be wonderful, but might not be the best choices for first-time pet owners. This lively chapter book is written on the fourth-grade reading level for kids 8-12.

In general, these creatures are bred in captivity as pets, widely-available and proven kid-pleasers.

However, you should know that some pets are not legal in some cities, states or provinces. Check local laws or restrictions online, by asking your vet or at a rescue shelter, such as The Humane Society or SPCA. Pet rescues are also where you can find healthy, socialized pets in need of a caring home.

Before adopting a pet, be sure to have a veterinarian lined up. They need to be a vet who's experienced with small pets and the specific pet you choose (unless this pet is a fish. Pet store staff are usually knowledgeable about fish ailments and treatments).

This book tells you about each pet, what it's like to have them and why they'd be a fun pet for young pet owners.

Generally, the pets in this book and all pets aren't suitable for very young children unless you can constantly monitor the safety of both child and pet.

Once you and your child (or class) have chosen the best pet, you'll want to do more reading about this pet's diet, housing and health needs.

This book is designed to be the starting point, introducing children, or any first-time pet owner, to all the best small fun pets there are and what it's like to have them.

We are pet owners, not veterinarians. Nothing included in this book is meant to serve as medical advice. If you suspect your pet is ill, please see your local vet. We accept no liability concerning your pet ownership.

Contents

CHAPTER 1 - SMALL FUN PETS FOR BEGINNING PET OWNERS 9

CHAPTER 2 - GOLDFISH 11

CHAPTER 3 - BETTA FISH 15

CHAPTER 4 - LEOPARD GECKO...............................19

CHAPTER 5 - BUDGIE, OR PARAKEET 22

CHAPTER 6 - CANARY 25

CHAPTER 7 - HAMSTER 29

CHAPTER 8 - GUINEA PIG OR CAVY 33

CHAPTER 9 - GERBIL 37

CHAPTER 10 - MOUSE 43

CHAPTER 11 - RAT...47

CHAPTER 12 - KITTEN OR CAT 52

CHAPTER 13 - PETS THAT AREN'T GOOD FOR BEGINNING PET OWNERS 59

CHAPTER 14 - GOOD CARE FOR YOUR NEW PET......63

CHAPTER 15 - WHAT PET WILL YOU GET?...............67

THANK YOU FOR READING! 69

SMALL FUN PETS

Chapter 1

Small Fun Pets for Beginning Pet Owners

Do you wish your family or your room at school could get a fun pet? Do you already know what pet you want most and why?

Should it be a cute pet?

A fluffy pet?

A pet that can ride around in your pocket and go everywhere you do?

A pet that understands words?

Or a pet that can learn to do tricks?

You have several types of pets to choose from. In this book, you'll meet pets that are the very best for beginning pet owners. All these pets are interesting to get to know.

All are easy for kids to care for, with just a bit of help from someone older like a parent or your teacher.

SMALL FUN PETS

A happy hamster dinner.

Photo Credit: Lichtpuenktchen via pixabay

There are lots of ways to have fun with these pets. You can give them a name, make their tank or cage a cool place to be, build them a pet playground or just hang out together.

So, are you ready to meet the fun pets who want to be your new best friend? The first one is orange and finny…

Chapter 2
Goldfish

Goldfish are the most popular pet in the world! They're colourful, interesting and they can even learn tricks!

Many people think goldfish are the easiest possible pet to have. Just get a bowl, put in some water and add a fish. Nothing could be easier, these people say!

Not true!

If you do this, your goldfish won't live for very long. Here's why. A goldfish bowl simply doesn't have enough water for goldies to get all the oxygen they need to survive. It also doesn't give them nearly enough space to live in and explore.

Goldfish are eating machines! They need to be, because goldfish have no stomach. So, they eat (and poop) a lot! This means you must be careful to give them the right amount of food and keep their water clean.

2 goldfish in an aquarium.

Photo Credit: Gemmiti via pixabay

Fish bowls are goldfish killers!

If you want goldfish that are healthy, they need to live in an aquarium with enough space for them and a filter to clean the water.

Goldfish also need a heater with their tank, to keep the water the temperature they like. And you will need to buy special chemicals for the water to help them stay healthy.

You'll need a 10-gallon aquarium, which is big enough for six tiny baby goldfish. If you want your pet goldfish to grow bigger, you should have only one or two goldfish in a 10-gallon (38 litre) tank. When they get to be 4 inches (10 cm.) long, they need to move to a bigger tank.

CHAPTER 2 - GOLDFISH

Goldfish aren't all gold. They can be black, brown, red, white or yellow, as well as orange. If they have one tail they are called comets. If they have two tails, they are called fantails.

They can be all one colour, or speckled in two or three colours. The ones that are many colours are called calico goldfish.

How much fun are goldfish?

Goldfish are interesting to watch as they swim around. You can also have fun setting up the tank, with an underwater scene or maybe play castles to swim in and out of or other fishy toys.

If you want plants in the tank, use plastic ones. Real plants won't last very long in your goldfish aquarium, because your pet will eat them.

They like dried fish food, but really get excited when you give them brine shrimp or tubifex worms (get these at pet stores) or ants, flies or spiders you catch in summer. They also love bits of raw hamburger or fresh lettuce.

Your goldfish pet can learn to recognize you as their owner, swimming toward you to say, "Hi" or going to the water surface when they see you to beg for food (they're always hungry, especially for treats).

Once they get to know you, they'll even take food from your hand!

Goldfish can learn tricks!

Goldfish are surprisingly intelligent. They have good memories.

13

Goldfish can recognize sounds, music and colours. They enjoy getting attention from their owners and like it when you change their tank around often.

Give them lots of things to explore. When goldfish get plenty of attention and an interesting tank to live in, they are healthier and live longer.

With good care, a pet goldfish can live as long as 50 years, which is much longer than almost any other pet!

How do you start?

For their first trick, teach your goldfish to eat from your fingers.

Begin by just tickling the water at the surface. Do this at the same time each day. In a few days, your goldfish will rush up to the surface, mouth open for food. Keep doing this and soon your goldfish will let you drop food right into his or her mouth!

Next, you could teach your goldfish to come when you call their name, play fetch, or play soccer, using a ping pong ball.

Like all pets, goldfish want to see you and spend some time together every day for at least half an hour.

Chapter 3
Betta Fish

Some pets are fun because they're friendly and you can hang out together.

Others do silly things that make you laugh. Or they can learn to do tricks.

Then there are the pets that can't hang out with you or do many tricks but they're still cool pets because they are fascinating to watch. They are just so different from people, you'll wonder what it would be like to be them.

Most fish don't make very good pets. They're too large, or too tricky to keep healthy, or just boring. But none of that is true of betta fish, the easiest, most colourful and most interesting pet fish you could have.

Bettas are spectacularly colourful. Usually, their tail is one bright colour and their body is another. They can be blue, red, orange, yellow, purple, gold, turquoise-green, black, blueish-white or pinkish-white.

Bettas can live for about five to 10 years.

A beautiful betta displaying his fins.

They were first found in Siam, a country in Asia that is now called Thailand. You can't have two male bettas in the same tank, because they will fight until one or both are so hurt that they die. But it's safe to have two female bettas in the same tank.

Because of the fighting, and where they're from, bettas are also known as *Siamese Fighting Fish*.

Some people think that bettas are fine living alone in just a fish bowl, but, like goldfish, they will be unhappy in such a small space. They won't live for very long.

A 10-gallon (38 liter) tank is big enough for your betta and a few tank friends. Here are some interesting types of fish that can live safely with bettas:

- Neon tetras and ember tetras – but keep a close eye on them. Some tetras like to bite other fish.

- Blue gouramis (but you will need a 20-gallon or 77-liter tank because they need a lot of space).

- Ghost shrimp. Get big ones or your betta will think they're a snack!

- African dwarf frogs.

- Bristlenose plecos, cory catfish or glass catfish.

- Common guppies. The coloured guppies are more interesting, but bettas will attack anything that is brightly coloured, so it's safer to choose the plainer guppies.

Bettas don't eat plants, so you can put some interesting real plants in your fish tank. And these fish like to stay warm, so you'll need a tank heater.

Here's what they eat: two to six betta fish pellets per day. Once a week they can have a treat of freeze-dried brine shrimp, bloodworms or black worms.

Be careful to feed your betta only as much food as it wants to eat in two minutes.

How to have fun with your betta

Put a clean ping pong ball on the surface of the tank water and most bettas will come up to play with it. They'll push it around in a game of fishy soccer. Don't leave the ball in there all the time because your pet will get bored with it.

Another way to have fun with your betta is by holding a mirror up to the side of their tank. They will think they're seeing another betta and flare, which means puff themselves up.

You can also find betta fish toys at the pet store that combine a ball and a mirror. Don't let your fish play with a mirror for more than five minutes or so because longer than that will exhaust your pet.

They also like to play with floating decorations. One of these is a betta log they can swim through. Some bettas like to sleep in their betta log. You can find betta logs at pet supply stores and online.

Bettas enjoy having fake or real plants in their tanks. They also really like it when their tank set-up is always changing and when things outside their tank change.

Betta pet tricks

Here's an easy way to keep them happy. Get some dry-erase markers and draw on the glass of their tank. You can do words, or doodles, or anything you want. Your betta will come right over to investigate!

When you're done playing, just erase and draw something else another time.

Or you could cut shapes out of sticky notes and put them on the sides of your fish tank. Bettas love bright colours and they like to chase anything that moves, including coloured shapes.

Bettas are one of the most intelligent species of fish. They can recognize their owners and some even learn simple tricks like pushing their toy ball through a hoop.

Chapter 4

Leopard Gecko

Has your family ever gone on vacation to Mexico, or other countries in Central America or South America? If so, you might have seen little green geckos and thought aren't they cute little guys! I bet they'd make a great pet!

Well, no, they wouldn't, because they're wild geckos and completely happy to be a wild creature. But those cute little green geckos have some tame cousins called leopard geckos, or leos for short. Leos are the cutest and friendliest little reptile pet there is.

They get their name – leopard – because they grow up to have yellow skin with brown leopard spots on their backs.

Like pet mice, leos are naturally quite shy. They are sweet and friendly once they get to know you. You can have fun designing their home and changing it around often, because they do get bored living in the same old tank.

Leopard geckos, like all reptile pets, don't do any tricks. But leos can learn to climb into your hand. If

Leopard geckos love big rocks to rest on.

you let them, they'll race up your front to sit on your shoulder.

Be careful they don't jump and fall!

With loving care, a little leo will never get very big, but they could live for a long time, as much as 25 years!

Leos are active in the morning and evening and sometimes at night. They mostly snooze during the day.

They make a good pet for beginning pet owners because they are friendly, sweet and happy being pets. They don't get very big, so you don't need a lot of space for their tank. They are hardy little creatures and easy to keep healthy.

A good home for a gecko

A 10-gallon (38 liter) or 20-gallon (76 liter) tank makes a good home for a leopard gecko.

They will also need a heating pad under their tank or a heat lamp, water and food dishes and places to hide, get warmer or cool off.

Leos eat live insects. Unlike birds and other reptiles, they don't ever eat plants or vegetables.

Geckos can lose their tails

One very strange thing leopard geckos do sometimes is lose their tails! This happens when they are frightened. Their tail just drops off and they run away, hoping that their enemy will be interested in eating their tail, not them!

Amazingly, the tail does grow back, but the new tail will be stubby and not nearly as nice-looking as their original tail.

Chapter 5
Budgie, or Parakeet

Parakeets are a small member of the parrot family.

One type of parakeet is called the budgerigar, or budgie for short. Wild budgies live in Australia.

All pet budgies are bred in captivity, which means their parents were pets. They are raised by hand to be pets.

This is important, because a hand-raised budgie can be a wonderful pet. Wild birds, like most wild animals, don't make good pets. They'd rather be wild.

One reason people enjoy budgies is their bright colours. They can be turquoise, dark blue, green, purple, gold or yellow. Almost all budgies can learn to whistle! And some, like their parrot cousins, can learn to say a few words.

Budgies, like all parrots, have a lot of personality! They like people and are very friendly. You can teach them commands, like "Step up!" when you want them to perch on your hand, or "Step down!" when you put them back in their cage.

CHAPTER 5 - BUDGIE, OR PARAKEET

A budgie resting on a perch.

Photo Credit: James DeMers via pixabay

Budgies need a large cage to live in, and they also need to spend some time every day out of their cage. Parakeets are very sensitive to smells, so they shouldn't ever live in a kitchen or any place where there are strong odours.

These 2 budgies are friends.

With good care, your budgie will live for a long time. Pet budgies typically live until they are eight or nine years old.

They eat bird pellets, birdseed and like to have some dark leafy greens. Give them a treat of apple, banana or melon slices once a week.

Budgies love their toys! They also enjoy a warm bird bath two or three times a week.

Chapter 6
Canary

Canaries are bright yellow birds, like Tweetie Pie in the Tweetie and Sylvester cartoons.

But did you know that not all canaries are yellow and not all of them can sing?

Wild canaries were first discovered living in the Canary Islands, which are in the Atlantic Ocean, just west of Morocco in Africa. All wild canaries are greenish-yellow. They got their name from their island home. Today, pet canaries can be bright yellow, orange, red, pink, white or a bluish-gray.

Pet canaries with the brightest colours are called *Border* canaries. *Choppers* are the ones able to sing a clear, high and loud song. Choppers always sing with their beaks open. Canaries with a quieter song, who always sing with their beaks closed, are called *Rollers*.

Female canaries can also be Borders, but they aren't able to sing. Instead, female canaries chirp or twitter.

People who want a bird with a spectacular colour and a beautiful song pay a lot of money for these

SMALL FUN PETS

A bright yellow canary.

special pets. Canaries you can buy at the pet store or find at a pet rescue are more likely to be females. All canaries make friendly, lively and intelligent pets.

Each male canary must learn his own song. Usually, he will start trying it out when he is about 12 weeks old, but he needs to practice a lot. He will be a year old before his song is perfect.

Male canaries always sing their song when they first wake up in the morning. Then they may sing it several more times during the day, until evening. They never sing at night because that's when they sleep.

CHAPTER 6 - CANARY

So why do boy canaries sing their beautiful songs? It might be to tell any other canaries that happen to be nearby, "Hey, I'm over here, and I know you'll like my song!"

Or it could be, "All you girl canaries out there, listen to this, because I want a girlfriend!"

Or it might just be, "I'm so happy, I just have to sing!"

Every canary you will meet wears a metal bracelet on one ankle, but this isn't just jewellery. The numbers stamped on the band tell you when this canary was born, so you can tell his or her age. With good care, pet canaries live for about nine to 15 years.

Some pet birds like to climb around their cage, but not canaries or parakeets. They're both fliers, so they need a cage that is big enough for them to be able to fly between their perches. To keep their feet and their perching skills strong, they need different sized perches. They also need a shallow dish of water because they love to splash in a birdbath.

Canaries, like any pet, get bored when they are locked up in a cage all the time. They need to get out every day for some play time with you and to fly around.

Before you let your pet canary out of their cage, you will need to canary-proof the room. Here's how to do it. Close the curtains and the door. Cover any mirrors or other windows with newspaper. You need to do this because your pet doesn't understand what a mirror or window is. They could fly into it and be seriously hurt.

Part of the fun of having a pet canary is setting up their home and giving them bird toys to play with. You can also teach them to step up onto your hand and step down from your hand when you are putting them back in their bird cage.

Here's what they eat. They want canary seed every day. They also need one boiled egg every day that is cooled and mashed up. Serve it to your pet in a separate cup, not with their birdseed.

They also enjoy small chunks of fruits and vegetables. You will soon learn which ones your pet likes the most. Some canaries love shredded carrots. Others would rather have a bit of apple or romaine lettuce. They should never have peanut butter or potatoes or corn.

Like all pets, canaries love treats! Here are their favourites: seed treats, egg cookies and spray millet. You can find all these at the pet store or order online. To stay healthy, your canary will also need a cuttlebone hung in their cage. It gives them the calcium they need to stay healthy.

Canaries are a happy, easy-going and fun small pet for kids age 8 and older. Like other small pets, you need to be gentle with them.

Unlike some other pets, you won't need to have two canaries, because they don't mind living alone so long as they get plenty of attention every day from their Best Pet Friend (that's you!)

Chapter 7

Hamster

Hamsters are chubby little guys with furry ears, short tails and wide feet.

They have fluffy, silky fur that can be black, silver-grey, golden, white, brown, yellow, red, apricot or a colour mix. Long-haired hamsters are called *fancy* or *teddy bear* hamsters.

Hamsters can't see very well and they are colour-blind. They rely on their excellent senses of smell and hearing to find food or avoid enemies.

They eat hamster food and like treats of seeds, nuts, greens, shredded carrots and apples.

One strange thing about hamsters is they are food hoarders. They store food in their cheeks and hide it in their cages.

There are many types of hamsters, but the pet hamsters you will most often see are either *Syrian* hamsters or *Dwarf* hamsters. Syrian hamsters grow

Hamsters can be great friends.

Photo Credit: Meditations via pixabay

up to be about 7 inches (17.7 cm.) long. Dwarf hamsters are about half that big when they are adults.

Don't put two hamsters together, because they will fight.

Hamsters like to be active in the morning and evening, and mostly snooze during the day. They can be very grumpy if you wake them up suddenly. If you try to play with them when they're eating or sleeping, or if you are playing too roughly, they get upset and might bite you.

Something cute that they do is wash their faces with their paws.

They like tunnels and any kind of paper tube or box to play with or hide in. You could give them milk paper cartons, old socks or scraps of soft fabric along with shredded paper towels or shredded newspaper for their nest.

They can live in a hamster cage, but you can also use a glass tank with a mesh top. Give them a hamster ball or hamster wheel and chew sticks to keep their teeth healthy.

Hamsters are good climbers. They'll be happy to ride around in your pocket or on your shoulder, but they aren't very good at hanging on. You'll have to hold them to be sure they don't fall.

Most pet hamsters live until they're two or three years old.

If you live in a city and want to see lots of different hamster pets, find out if there'll be a hamster show coming up soon that you and your family could go to. That's where hamster breeders and owners show off their pets and enter them in 'Best Hamster' contests. It's also where you can learn more about hamsters and find your new pet.

SMALL FUN PETS

This black cavy is a short-hair.

Chapter 8
Guinea Pig or Cavy

Have you ever seen a pet that looks like a walking dust mop? If so, this pet is a shaggy, long-haired guinea pig, or cavy.

Guinea pigs, or cavies, were first found as wild animals in the Andes Mountains of Peru, South America.

They have a lot to say to their owners. When you're giving them a scratch behind the ears, they'll purr, just like a kitten or cat.

They aren't pigs, but they oink, honk, snort, wheek and whistle when they're happy to see you and squeal when they want food. They can growl when they're scared. The babies chirp when they are frightened or hungry.

They have thick fur. Their coat can be pure white, black, ginger, gold, or brown. Some have short hair, and some are so shaggy you can't see their feet.

Like a long-haired cat or dog, the shaggy guinea pigs need to be brushed every day. Use a metal comb

SMALL FUN PETS

Guinea pigs love to play outside.

Photo Credit: Vantagepointfl via pixabay

or bristle brush. You only need to brush a shorthair cavy once a week. All guineas also need a bath once a week or so, in warm water with a bit of baby shampoo in it.

Just like cats, guinea pigs are snackers. They like to have little meals all day long. They eat guinea pig pellets and need timothy hay every day. They like treats of apples, beets, corn, lettuce, carrots, flowers or leaves.

In warm weather, you can take them out to play. They'll be happy to have a taste of fresh grass.

Like other rodent pets, cavies need chew twigs to keep their teeth healthy.

They also like their own guinea pig playground. You can make one out of wood, or cardboard boxes, with ramps and platforms.

They also love a fleece forest. Just cut out some scraps of fleece fabric, hang them from a wire grid and place that over your guinea's play space. An old child's playpen works for a guinea pig play space. You can cut up old sweat shirts for the fleece, or buy fleece remnants at a fabric and sewing store.

Guineas also like pipe structures to crawl through and love to play with paper bags. Just don't give them a hamster wheel. They're too big to fit in it and, if they try using the wheel, they could hurt their backs or legs.

Cavies need space that is bigger than a tank. They want a hutch big enough for two, because they need to live with a cavy friend. Getting two females that are the same age works the best.

You need a floor on your hutch, not just wire, because wire will cause guineas to get a foot infection, called *bumblefoot*, that is painful. Paper or corn cob bedding is the best.

Of all the rodent pets, guinea pigs are the most loving towards their owners. They usually live four or five years, but some can get to be 10 years old with good care.

Cavies can't do any tricks. They're a fun pet because they love playing with their toys and hanging out with you. They can also learn to get along with other family pets, especially cats. It's safe to let them

SMALL FUN PETS

Guinea pigs make for very cuddly friends.

Photo Credit: Vickypawprints via pixabay

out to play because, unlike other small pets, guinea pigs don't try to hide or escape.

Sweet, friendly and with lots of personality, cavies make a good beginning pet-owner pet!

Chapter 9
Gerbil

Little gerbils look like hamsters, but when you get to know them, you'll discover that gerbils can do some cool things that hamsters can't.

They're the same size as hamsters. They're just as curious as hamsters or mice. But they're a lot more laid-back than mice and a lot less bitey than hamsters.

They can be gray, brown or multi-colour. Most gerbils have a long tail with a tuft of fur at the tip, but *dupraise* gerbils have short, fat tails with no tuft.

Originally known as desert rats or sand rats, their natural home is an arid place (*arid* means it almost never rains there).

Gerbils have adapted to be healthy in their dry home countries. This means gerbils hardly ever pee or poop. They are a clean creature that has no smell, something you can't say about almost any other pet!

Kids who have gerbils also like them because you don't have to clean their tank as often as some other pets.

SMALL FUN PETS

One cute thing gerbils can do is stand up and beg.

Gerbils love peanuts.

Photo Credit: Meditations via pixabay

Can gerbils do tricks?

Yes. Here's a trick gerbils can do that most other pets can't. Just like their very distant cousins, chipmunks and squirrels, gerbils can stand up on their hind legs.

And here's another cute thing they do. When they get excited, they thump their back legs on the ground.

Gerbils love toys. Give them any type of paper tube, like one from toilet paper or paper towels (kitchen roll) and they'll be happy. More than any other rodent pet, they love hanging out with their owner. They're perfectly happy riding along in your pocket or the sleeve of your jacket, doing whatever you're doing.

Should you get one gerbil, or two?

Gerbils are very social, living in family groups when they're wild. They aren't happy as an only pet, living alone. Get two gerbils that are the same age and are both boys, or both girls and they will get along.

Some people put their gerbils in a hamster cage, but a 10-gallon (76 liter) tank is a better choice because they need more space and they need their paper bedding to be 3 inches (7.6 cm.) deep so they can burrow. The tank will need a mesh top, so they get plenty of fresh air but can't escape.

Wire cages aren't good because gerbils can kick some of their bedding out of the cage, making a mess. Also, they sometimes chew on the wire of a cage, injuring their mouths and teeth. Don't put your gerbils in a plastic cage. It will be too small and they will soon destroy it by chewing an escape hatch.

Gerbils also need a nest box for sleeping. A clay plant pot on its side works well for this. Give them plenty of shredded tissues or clean grass hay and they will build their bed inside the pot.

One way to have fun with your gerbils is to make them a gerbil playground. It could have some flat rocks to sit on, ladders, ramps and platforms. Another way is to take cute photos of your pets. They're hardly ever still long enough to get a great shot, except when they're eating or when they poke their head out of their nest.

CHAPTER 9 - GERBIL

Gerbils can be different colours. This one is black.

Photo Credit: Meditations via pixabay

Like all rodents, gerbils love to chew. Give them branches, wood or rope parrot toys. They also like small cardboard boxes for chewing.

Some gerbils really enjoy having an exercise wheel. If you get one, it needs to be the type that isn't the open wire frame type, because they can easily get their tail caught in it.

If you can't find one with a floor inside the wheel, you could get an open wire exercise wheel and make a floor for the wheel with cardboard and tape. Be sure there is no place in the wheel for your pet to get their tail stuck.

SMALL FUN PETS

This gerbil just woke up and is taking a look out his front door.

Gerbils like gerbil food. For treats, they like raw oatmeal, peanut butter, popcorn and fresh lettuce, carrots, zucchini, kale, apples or broccoli.

They usually live two to three years.

Chapter 10

Mouse

Have you ever heard the expression, "As timid as a mouse?"

It's true. Mice are timid little creatures. But they're also cute and curious little pets that like their owners, once they get to know them.

They're so tiny you can easily fit one in your hand. But because they are so small, even a little kid looks like a giant to them. Be careful not to frighten them!

Mice can't see very well. But they are very good at hearing things and at smelling things. They use their ears, nose and sense of taste to understand their world and everything in it.

You must be gentle when you hold a mouse. Any sudden loud sound or movement will make them leap out of your hand! If they fall to the floor they could easily be hurt.

A frightened mouse could also bite you.

A mouse that gets away will hide and be very hard to find.

SMALL FUN PETS

A friendly pet mouse.

Photo Credit: Auenleben via pixabay

Pet mice, also called fancy mice, can be many colours including black, chocolate brown, white, red, silver or gray. The ones that are all one colour are called *selfs*. Mice that are one colour on their back, but have a tan belly are called *tans*.

Mice are social animals, which means they don't like to be alone. It's best to get two mice pets to live together. When you do, it should be two girl mice because two boys will fight. And if you get one girl and one boy, there will soon be babies – a *lot* of babies. A mama mouse has as many as 15 mouse pups at a time!

Pet mice love having a hamster wheel in their home, but don't put your mouse, or your mouse sisters in a hamster cage. It's just too small for them!

CHAPTER 10 - MOUSE

Always be gentle when handling a mouse.

A 20-gallon (75 litre) glass aquarium with a mesh cover makes a good house for your mice. It will need bedding on the floor, ladders to two or three stages for your pets to climb to, exercise wheels and plenty of toys!

Pet mice love old cardboard tubes (like the ones from toilet paper), small cardboard boxes, paper egg cartons and anything else they can hide in.

Give them scraps of fabric, string, yarn and shredded paper and, overnight, they will build themselves a nest! In a few weeks, their old nest might get a bit smelly. When this happens, throw it away, give your pet more nest-building materials and they'll happily build themselves a new one!

One thing you should know about mice is they usually only live for a year or two.

Mice can't really learn any tricks, but you can train them to climb onto your hand, and then up to your shoulder. You do this by offering them little treats of fresh raw vegetables or little nibbles of meat or cheese. Pets always like the people who feed them!

Mice need to chew!

One amazing thing about mice is their teeth never stop growing! They must chew things to keep their teeth from getting too big to fit in their mouth!

To keep your pet from chewing on everything, give him or her a dog bone to chew on. Or get mouse chew sticks at the pet store.

When a mouse is having a snooze, they really don't want to wake up. If you would like to play with your sleeping mouse, take a cotton-tip stick and very gently stroke them on their back. Let them wake up gradually.

Just like loud noises, having to wake up suddenly makes a mouse want to bite someone. But if you are very gentle and kind to your little mouse, it will be a sweet, friendly and interesting pet!

Here's how to pick up a mouse. Begin by letting them sniff your hand, so they recognize you. Then, with one hand, gently hold their tail at the very base of their tail while scooping the mouse into your other cupped hand. Keep gently holding their tail so they won't jump away.

Soon they will learn to trust you and want to come to your hand for some time together.

Chapter 11

Rat

Have you ever wanted a clever pet that would be happy to hang out with you, riding around in your pocket and meeting all your friends?

If so, it could be the pet you want is a rat. They make a cool pet for kids because they have lots of personality, are easy to care for and they love to be handled and cuddled, once they get to know you.

Unfortunately, rats have a bad reputation for being dirty animals that live at the garbage dump and spread diseases. All this is true about wild rats.

Rats born to be pets are completely different. They are very clean, safe to have around and, unlike some other pets, they don't bite.

They might look like their tiny mouse cousins, but pet rats are calmer, friendlier and smarter than mice or hamsters. When you hold them, they don't try to escape, like mice or hamsters often do.

Pet rats can be all black, brown or gray. If they are all white with pink eyes, they are an *albino* rat. The ones

These pet rats are enjoying a pumpkin snack..

Photo Credit: Kira Hoffman via pixabay

that are two colours together such as tan and white or gray and white are called *hooded* rats.

Rats are a clean animal that can learn to use a litter box, so you can let them out to play in your home. Just be careful that they don't try to disappear underneath the sofa. If they do, tempt them back with a food treat.

Like all pets, sometimes they need a bit of help staying clean. If so, gently wash your pet rat with a soft cloth dipped in warm water with a little bit of baby shampoo added.

Some rats love to take a swim in your bathtub or a kiddy pool.

Though a rat looks like just a big mouse, they behave like a different animal. Rats are curious,

CHAPTER 11 - RAT

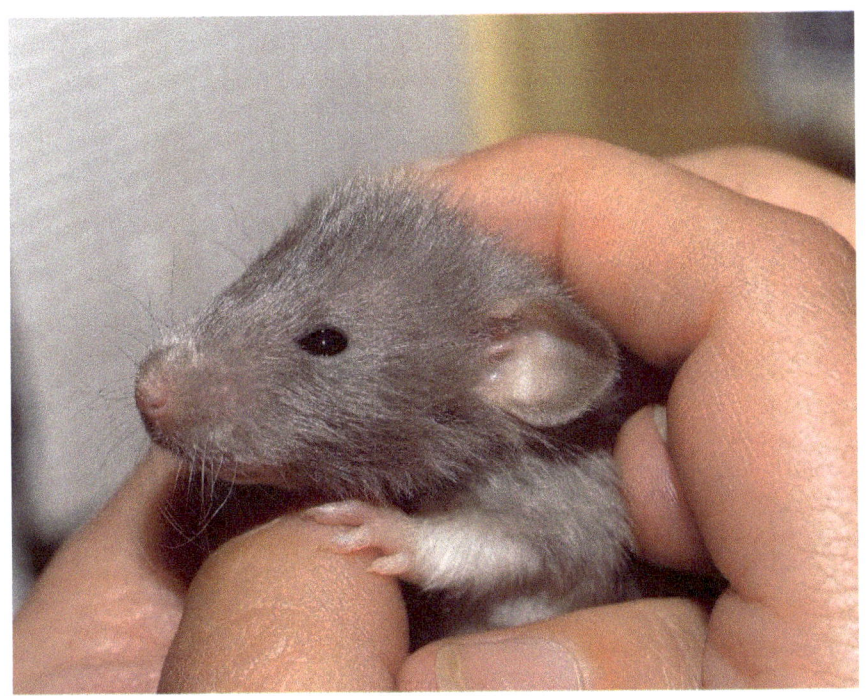

A baby rat.

Photo Credit: Kapa65 via pixabay

brave and friendly if they were raised from the time they were very small to be a pet.

When you choose your pet rat, try to get a girl, because female rats are more alert and less lazy than males. Some people also think the females are prettier.

Rats love to come out to play! They especially like riding around in the sleeve of your sweater or the pocket of your shirt, hanging out together and seeing what you like to do. They don't make a sound, and aren't jumpy.

Rats do squeak, but it is in ultra-sound, which people can't hear (but dogs and cats can). And they

SMALL FUN PETS

will bite, if they are frightened or you stick your finger into their cage.

Rats live for three or four years. This is longer than most rodent pets. With kindness and care, your pet could live much longer! There was a pet rat named Rodney who lived to be very old, for a rat. He was seven years and four months old when he died.

Here's what to feed your pet rat:

- Lab chow for rats, or
- Gerbil food, or
- Birdseed mixed with rabbit pellets.

Here's what they like for treats:

- Cheese
- Little pieces of meat
- Raw spinach
- Peanut butter
- Bananas

A 10-gallon (38 liter) tank can be home for a rat. It will need a mesh top. You will need to clean your rat's home less often if you choose a wire cage like a guinea pig cage or a ferret cage. These are the ideal size for a pet rat.

They also need some bones or dog chews to gnaw on and fabric scraps or shredded paper towels to make their nest.

Use cardboard boxes and paper towel tubes to make them a pet playground. You can have fun making mazes, ramps and climbing frames and stages.

Can rats do tricks?

Yes, you can teach your rat to do some tricks. They are so smart that they're easy to train.

Use food treats to train your rat. Here are some tricks they can learn:

- To climb up and sit on your shoulder.
- To come when you call them.
- To stand up or jump over an object.
- To use their litter box.
- To shake a paw.

Look on You Tube to find lots more awesome and amazing tricks you can teach your new pet rat!

Chapter 12
Kitten or Cat

Like people, cats have very individual personalities.

Some cats love to be cuddled. Others just don't want to be lap cats.

Some are very talky, while others hardly ever make a sound.

Some love to play and even do tricks, while others aren't interested and would rather snooze, or look out the window at birds.

Some are excellent hunters, so no mouse will ever get into your home. Others couldn't care less about hunting.

But the one thing all cats are is independent. They like knowing you're around, especially when their food dish is empty.

But they really don't mind being on their own. If they're left home alone all day, that's OK with them. They'll happily curl up and take a nap on the nearest

CHAPTER 12 - KITTEN OR CAT

This is a Siamese cat.

cushion or soft chair. Or in your closet, because they love warm, soft and cozy places to hide.

SMALL FUN PETS

Cats and people have been friends for thousands of years.

Cats have lived with people for longer than any other animal. But cats didn't always live with people as pets. At first, and for a very long time, all cats had a job.

Many thousands of years ago, people learned how to be farmers. They began raising crops of grains like wheat, oats and barley. People used these grains to make bread and other foods.

Grains were stored in barns until they were needed. Mice and rats thought these barns were a wonderful place to get all the free food they wanted, so they moved in!

Cats are meat eaters. The perfect cat-sized snack is a mouse. Since all the mice were hanging out in barns, cats decided this was a good place for them to hunt, so they moved into the barns, too!

Of course, people noticed this. They wanted to protect their crops and not let the mice eat it. Then they noticed how useful the cats were. Cats didn't want human food. Instead, they protected the grain so people could eat it. So, having cats in the barns was a smart idea.

The farmers got more cats, the cats ate more mice and rats, the grain was saved. Everyone was happy, except for the mice and rats that got eaten.

This went on for a very long time, until some children thought it might be nice to have kittens as pets. These kittens grew up to be cats that decided living in a nice warm house as a pet was even better than being a wild cat that lives in a barn.

And so, for a very long time, some cats have been working cats, protecting the grain in barns, but they are still wild. Others have lived mostly or entirely indoors as pets, enjoying an easy life.

Though most wild cats (also called *feral* cats) don't live very long, pampered pet cats usually live 12 to 16 years, and many into their 20s.

Today, pet cats can be many colours, including black, brown, ginger (reddish-blond) and white. They can also be mixed colours or patterns.

Almost all cats have white paws with five toes on their front paws and four toes on their back paws. All cats walk not on their feet, but on their toes!

SMALL FUN PETS

These kittens are just a few weeks old.

Photo Credit: Klaus Juntke via pixabay

They can have short hair and a smooth coat, or be fluffy, with long hair. There are even cats with no hair at all, bred to be safe for people who are allergic to all other types of cats or dogs.

Kittens are usually very active and playful, running around, getting into mischief and doing lots of crazy things that make you laugh. They like to play with balls, pounce on things that move and climb up your legs to sit in your lap. But not for long, because kittens are very active, always racing around!

Fairly quickly kittens grow up to be cats, who run and play in short bursts of energy before settling down for another nap.

Cats easily learn to use a litter box, which must be cleaned every day.

They are snackers, so they like always having food in their dish. Healthy adult cats eat dried cat food. Kittens need their mother's milk first, then they learn to eat wet cat food (it comes in cans) and finally, dry cat food.

Cats learn how to hunt and kill birds and mice or rats from their mothers. When this learning doesn't happen, a pet cat can live with pet mice or a pet rat and might chase them, but they won't know how to kill them.

What tricks can cats do?

Pet cats can do some amazing things.

They can learn their name and come when you call them.

They are amazing jumpers and can get to the top of the refrigerator or the highest shelf in a room. They like to sit there and look down on their world.

They can climb up trees, but not all cats have learned how to climb down again.

They always land on their feet, because when a cat falls, it swivels its tail and turns its body in mid-air.

Most cats don't like water, but they do know how to swim and some cats even like it.

Most cats really don't enjoy car rides. But many are quite happy riding around with you in your backpack or going for a walk on a leash.

And some are amazing acrobats, able to learn to jump up and do a complete back-flip or leap through hoops!

All cats like any toy that looks like a mouse. If it moves like a mouse, that's even more interesting, if you're a cat! And if that mouse toy is filled with catnip, some cats will just go crazy, rolling around, leaping about and making happy cat noises.

Catnip is an herb, like mint. You can grow a little pot of it, dry it (like you would other herbs) and use it as stuffing for a cat toy. Catnip seeds are sold at gardening centres.

Or you can buy catnip cat toys at pet stores or online.

Kittens, and some cats, will play with almost anything you give them – a ball of yarn, a toilet paper roll, a ball, any small soft toy or even a piece of paper. Kittens especially like having a play house you make out of an upside- down cardboard box with a door cut in the side.

Chapter 13

Pets That Aren't Good For Beginning Pet Owners

There are some pets that really don't make good pets for kids. Or for anyone who's never had a pet before.

These might be pets that are wild creatures and really don't want to be pets, like wounded wild birds or a fawn that has lost its mother.

And there are some other pets that easily get sick and die. Or require a lot of work to keep them healthy. Or cost a lot of money.

Maybe you will choose to have some of these pets when you're older and more experienced as a responsible pet owner.

Here are some of the pets that just aren't right, as beginning pets for kids or first-time pet owners:

1. **Turtles**. The little baby turtles you see at the pet shop are cute, but they easily get sick and die.

2. **Tropical fish**. All tropical fish live in saltwater.

A pet leopard gecko exploring his cage.

Saltwater is the same as the water in the ocean.

Setting up a saltwater tank is more complicated than a tank for freshwater fish, like goldfish and bettas.

Tropical fish can be very exotic and beautiful, but they usually cost a lot of money. So does everything you need to keep them healthy.

3. **Ferrets** have lots of personality. But they also have sharp claws and can be quite smelly. In many places, it's against the law to have one as

CHAPTER 13 - PETS THAT AREN'T GOOD FOR BEGINNING PET OWNERS

a pet. They can be as affectionate as a kitten or cat and can learn to use a litter box, so they can be a good pet, but aren't a brilliant pet for kids or for anyone who has never had a pet before.

4. **Snakes**. All snakes are reptiles, so they need to eat live food, like mice or birds. There are some types of snakes that aren't poisonous or dangerous to have.

   One problem with snakes is that they eat their food when it is still alive, which some people find upsetting.

   Also, all snakes are escape artists. They are always trying to get out of their enclosure or tank and have a little look around your home or classroom. This can be very scary for someone who isn't expecting to see a snake wandering around!

5. There are some **reptiles** that don't mind being pets, like the leopard gecko in this book. But the thing to remember about lizard pets is that they eat live insects, so you will have crickets and worms in your home or classroom. You will need to look after these insects until they become food for your lizard pet. There is no way to make crickets stop making cricket noises, just about all the time.

   Reptile pets also require heat lamps, humidity control (this is how much moisture there is in the air) and other things that can make them too difficult a pet for beginning pet owners, unless there's an adult that does most of the pet care.

6. **Dogs** can be wonderful pets, but they aren't a good first pet. Here's why. Dogs need a LOT of attention. They need at least one good walk every day and two walks is better. Depending on the breed, they can be expensive to buy and to feed. All dogs are unpleasant to live with unless they are trained. This training takes skill and time.

Dogs are miserable when they are left alone because dogs are a social animal. They're used to living with other dogs or with people. They can get very anxious when left alone. When they are anxious, they might bark and howl, or have accidents on the carpet, or destroy things.

When they do this, they aren't being bad dogs. They're just telling their owners that they are very stressed and need more attention and care. This is usually too much for one kid to do without a lot of help from brothers and sisters or from adults.

Dogs live for about 10 years, but some can live for 20 years. If you really want a dog, and can give him or her a loving home for a long time, here are the most easy-going, kid-friendly types of dogs to get:

- Labrador Retrievers
- Golden Retrievers
- Boxers
- Beagles

Chapter 14

Good Care for Your New Pet

The things that every pet needs to be healthy and happy are a lot like the things that every kid needs to be healthy and happy.

These things are clean water, a safe and comfortable home, healthy food, kind and loving care and, if they get sick, medical care.

Before you get your new pet, you will want to think about how you are going to give him or her all these things that every pet needs:

1. **Fresh water**. Pets need clean, fresh water to drink and their water needs to be changed every day.

    If your pet is a fish, they need clean water in their tank and sometimes you will need to add more water so the tank is full. You will also need to test the water to be sure it is safe for your fish.

SMALL FUN PETS

A girl playing with her guinea pig.

Photo Credit: Pezibear via pixabay

If you live in a town or city and you get your water from a tap (faucet), it might have chlorine in it. This is a chemical used to make water safe for people to drink, but it is not healthy for pets.

To get rid of the chlorine, put the water in a bowl and let it sit for half an hour (most of the chlorine will evaporate, which means go out into the air).

For fish pets, you can buy water conditioner tablets that take the chlorine out of water before you add it to your fish tank. Buy these at a pet store or online.

2. The **right food**, in the right amount. This means don't give them too little or too much. Just like people, pets want to get their food at the same

time each day. They feel better knowing when they're going to get fed!

3. **Give them treats and toys**. Mice, rats, gerbils and hamsters all need twigs, chew sticks or bones to gnaw on. They also need the right bedding in their cage or tank. Any type of wood shavings can make them sick (and could kill them). Instead, use clean shredded paper.

4. A **regular routine**. Pets want to know when it is time to play with you, when it's quiet time for them to rest or sleep and when it's time for treats!

5. **Attention**. Pets like people and like to spend time with you. If you ignore your pet, he or she will get bored. For some types of pets, being bored a lot can make them sick or could even kill them. Pets want to hang out with their owners at least one hour every day.

6. A **clean, comfortable home**. Make sure their home is safe for your pet. It needs to be large enough and have places for them to rest or sleep. There needs to be a place in their tank or cage where they can go to be alone sometimes.

   Mice, rats, gerbils and hamsters want to make their own nests. Give them an old sock, tissues, a washcloth or paper towels. They also like a shoe box with a hole cut in it for a door as a place to hide in.

7. **Toys**. All pets need something interesting to play with – just like kids do!

8. **Temperature control**. Like people, pets want to be not too hot and not too cold.

9. **Be gentle** when you handle your pet! They are smaller than you and are easily hurt if you aren't careful! And remember, any pet will scratch you, bite or try to get away when they are frightened or you are hurting them.

   Pick them up gently with both hands. Never try to pick them up by their tail or one leg. If they don't want to be held right now, gently put them back in their tank or cage.

10. Pets rely on you to be a **responsible pet parent**. This means taking them to the veterinarian (animal doctor) when they're ill, unless they're a fish. When your fish is sick, ask what to do at the pet store.

11. **Wash your hands** with soap and warm water before and after you touch any pet! Just like people, pets can have germs that can make you sick. And you might have some germs that could make your pet sick! But this won't happen if you **always** remember to wash your hands before you touch your pet and after you play with them. This is true for every kind of pet.

Doing all these simple things, every day, will help give your pet what every pet wants - a long and healthy life.

It will mean you and your small fun pet enjoy lots of happy times together and you both stay safe!

Chapter 15
What Pet Will You Get?

So, what is the best small fun pet for you?

If you want a **quiet pet**, choose a betta fish, goldfish, gerbil or rat.

If you want a **pocket pet**, choose a gerbil, rat, mouse or hamster.

If you want a **furry pet**, choose a gerbil, guinea pig, kitten or cat.

If you want a pet that's **fun to play with**, choose a gerbil, rat, kitten or cat.

If you want a pet that **likes to hang out with you**, choose a parakeet, gerbil, guinea pig, rat, kitten or cat.

If you want a pet that **understands words**, choose a parakeet, rat or cat.

If you want an **unusual pet**, choose a leopard gecko.

If you are **allergic to pets**, choose a hairless cat or a leopard gecko.

SMALL FUN PETS

"Fish, delicious fish."

If you want a **smart pet**, choose a kitten, cat or rat.

If you need a pet that is **OK on its own for a few days** (like over the weekend in your classroom, or if you go away for two or three days), choose a pet rodent such as a mouse, rat, hamster or gerbil. Or, with enough food and water out and an extra litter box, a cat can be left alone and be perfectly content on its own for a few days.

THANK YOU for reading!

I hope you've enjoyed meeting the interesting and fun small pets in this book.

Do you know which one you want yet?

Once you choose your new pet, you'll want to learn LOTS more about them. To do this, you could go to pet shows, read about pets online, or read more pet books. There are so many interesting things to learn about pets, I know you'll have fun finding out about them and having them!

Wishing you many happy times with your new pet!

- *Jacquelyn*

About Jacquelyn

Jacquelyn Elnor Johnson writes books about pets for children. Her family has just one pet, a cat named Boots. But in the past, there have been many wonderful dogs in her life, including Dachshunds, Poodles and a black Labrador Retriever.

She and her family live in Nova Scotia, Canada.

THANK YOU FOR READING!

More fun pet and animal books you might like, all written for kids who are 9 to 12, or in grades three to seven:

Best Pets for Kids Series:

    I Want a Puppy, or a Dog

    I Want a Kitten, or a Cat

    I Want a Bearded Dragon

    I Want a Leopard Gecko

Fun Pets for Kids Series:

    Small Fun Pets; Beginner Pets for Kids 9-12

    Top 10 Fun Pets for Kids 9-12

Fun Animal Facts for Kids Series:

    Fun Dog Facts for Kids 9-12

    Fun Cat Facts for Kids 9-12

    Fun Leopard Gecko and Bearded Dragon Facts for Kids 9-12

    Fun Reptile Facts for Kids 9-12; Lizards, Turtles, Crocodilians, Snakes and Birds

Investigate more books for curious kids right here:

www.BestPetsForKids.fun

www.ingramcontent.com/pod-product-compliance
Lightning Source LLC
Chambersburg PA
CBHW061745290426

43673CB00095B/272